Journey Through Darkness

Journey Through Darkness

By Abbey DiGiando

iUniverse, Inc.

New York Lincoln Shanghai

Journey Through Darkness

iUniverse books may be ordered through booksellers or by contacting:

iUniverse
2021 Pine Lake Road, Suite 100
Lincoln, NE 68512
www.iuniverse.com
1-800-Authors (1-800-288-4677)

ISBN-13: 978-0-595-40537-4 (pbk)
ISBN-13: 978-0-595-84902-4 (ebk)
ISBN-10: 0-595-40537-1 (pbk)
ISBN-10: 0-595-84902-4 (ebk)

Printed in the United States of America

—For Mike

—A.N.D.

Contents

PART III   MY ADVICE

Acknowledgements

I would like to thank all of the people in my life that made not only this book possible for me, but my recovery as well. Especially: Mark DiGiando, Theresa DiGiando, Kaylee DiGiando, Jordan DiGiando, Janice Lemmons, Robert Lemmons, Mike Heinmiller, Olga Treskunova, Katie Hathaway, Brittiania Novotney, Carrie Feldman, Carly Esposito, Michelle Biedenbach, Kory Blair, Cody Moore, Patrick McAvena, Michael Burgess, Matt Malone, Dan Kaylor, Kim Louks, Jody Fournier, Ph.D., Kerm Almos, Ph.D., Rich Ashbrook, Ph.D., and Mike Torello, Ph.D.

In addition to my friends and family who formed a great support system and provided me with a great deal of encouragement, I would like to thank my doctors for all of their help in my diagnosis and treatment.

I would also like to thank all of the wonderful people at Studio 187, especially Corey, for the substantial amount of time they spent with me designing the cover and author photo for this book.

Finally I would like to thank Dr. Kevin Griffith for his guidance and kindness in helping me achieve my personal goals as a writer.

—A.N.D.

Note from the Author

When I was first diagnosed with major depression, I did not really know where to turn. I got the medical attention that I needed, but I felt very alone in what I was going through. I started reading books about depression, but I got tired of reading about the causes of depression and chemical imbalances. I felt like all the authors cared about was all of the medical and psychological factors associated with depression. The person who suffers from depression seemed to be left out of the equation.

I feel that to truly understand depression you must understand what a person with depression goes through. When I wrote this book I wanted to tell about my personal battle with depression. I want people to understand that depression is more than a chemical imbalance, and that those who suffer are not alone.

In addition to my personal story, I want people to understand that people who suffer from depression are suffering from a real illness, and that not all suffers are affected by depression in the same way. Also, society tells us that being depressed is shameful. This is the one thing that I would like to stress the most; if you feel that you may be suffering from depression, don't feel ashamed. Depression affects more people than you may think.

It is my hope that this book helps people gain a better understanding of what depression is really like. This book is biased because it is my story and should not be generalized to all cases of depression. When reading this story please know that I wrote this book in a very specific way; I will often talk to you directly. I want you the reader to feel as if you are in the room with me and I am telling you my story.

In order to protect their identity, the names and details of several characters in this memoir has been changed.

PART I
My Battle

Growing Up

"See ya on saturdoo grandma!" I said into my grandpa's camera, as I was saying goodbye after lunch. I was three years old and loved life. I loved spending time with my family. As a young girl, I was very interested in the world around me. I was curious. On one occasion I was in a restaurant with my mom, dad, grandma, grandpa, and my sister, and all of the sudden I stood up and asked, "How do you get out of this place?" My environment was very important, even when I was three. I wanted to know the rhyme and reason behind everything that I experienced. My mind has always been going. At 19 months I was blessed with a new baby sister, Kaylee. Although I do not remember her birth, I remember growing up with her.

As a young girl, I was very close to my sister; we did everything together. It was almost as if we were twins. I never remember my life without her. In addition to sharing all of my experiences with my sister, my mom was also a common factor in our experiences. I was very fortunate because my mom quit her job to stay home and raise us. I am eternally grateful for her sacrifice.

When I look back on my childhood, I remember all of the things that my mom did for us. When I was much younger, I was allowed to fill baking pans up with flour and play in it. I still remember the smooth feeling of the flour running between my fingers. I made such a mess, but I had a great time.

Kaylee and I always had a great time when we were growing up. I will never forget the time that my mom let us build a house in our basement, "Let's build a family room." said Kaylee.

"Yeah and lets build a kitchen too!" I said. After much *hard* labor our house was complete.

"I love it." Kaylee whispered.

"Me too"

"I think that we need a TV in our family room." Kaylee suggested.

"How about some lamps?" I added.

"I think that would be a great idea," my mom said as she found some old lamps in the garage sale pile. "Do you think these would work?" she asked us. Kaylee and I thought that the lamps were great. Then my mom suggested that we get some end tables to put the lamps on. Kaylee and I thought that would be a great idea.

When our family room was completed the three of us moved onto our babies nursery, "I think that we should put a few cribs in here, because our babies will want to take naps." Kaylee said.

"I think that we should have two rocking chairs, too." I added. After the nursery was completed, Kaylee, my mom, and I moved onto the classroom, and then the kitchen adding our own personal touches here and there. Finally, Kaylee and I sat down on the couch in our new family room and watched some TV. Our house was now a home.

Kaylee and I built our house in our basement by hanging sheets from the ceiling. Our home was complete with a kitchen, a family room with a TV and couch, a hallway, two bedrooms, a classroom with real school desks and a chalkboard, a library, and a baby nursery. It was so much fun; I'll never forget those days.

Whenever the weather was nice Kaylee and I got to play outside. We had our own little washing machine and dryer and we would wash all of our dolls cloths. We also had a swimming pool and a sandbox. If we were not playing in the house, swimming, or playing in the sandbox, we could be found at one of our neighbors' houses. The houses that surrounded our house all had kids that were around our age. There was a girl to the left of my parents house and her name was April, to the left of her house was a boy named John, and to the left of his house was another little girl named Anna. It's safe to say that we were never bored. We would spend our days playing house and sometimes we would play with the boys. "Watch out!" I screamed to April. We were playing war.

"Quick, help me build some more missiles." Kaylee and I gathered up all of the mud that our little hands could hold and shaped it into little round balls that we used as missiles.

Kaylee and I had a lot of fun as young kids. Our mom was always there when we were growing up. I have a lot of memories of the time she spent with us. My dad, however, had to work a lot for my mom to be able to stay home with us. Somehow, even when I was a young girl, I understood why my dad was not there as much as some of my friends' dads. I understood that he was working to support our family. Even though he did work a lot, I have very fond memories of my dad. "Are you girls ready?" he would ask us while we were getting ready to go see the Columbus Chill play. My dad always took us to hockey games. In addition to taking us out when he was off of work, my dad made every homecoming special.

"Daddy's home," my mom would say, and my sister and I would run to greet him. Almost every night when he would come home, he would bring all of us kids a treat. My parents spoiled all of us.

When I was seven years old my brother, Jordy, joined our family. For a five and a seven year old girl, having a real baby in the house was a dream come true. I will never forget the day that he was born. "Let's get in the tub," grandma said. She was getting us ready to go and meet our new baby brother for the very first time. I still remember walking outside, it was such a warm sunny day, and believe it or not, it was Mothers' Day. Kaylee and I put on our best little dresses and went to the hospital to meet our new brother.

"What do you girls think?" our mom asked us when we saw Jordy for the first time. I looked at Kaylee and just smiled, I saw her little blue eyes light up.

"Can I hold him?" I asked

"As long as you wash your hands and then sit on the couch." My mom said. Since I was the oldest I got to hold him first. I still remember, it was just like holding one of my dolls. However, this time he was real, he could look back at me, he was warm.

"When do I get to hold him?" Kaylee asked rather impatiently.

"Abbey, can Kaylee hold him now?" asked my mom. I said Okay. Kaylee washed her hands and sat down. My dad came and took Jordy from me and gave him to Kaylee. I watched her reaction, which I must say was very similar to my own. Her face again lit up; this was her real live baby doll as well. Kaylee and I never were jealous of our new bother. The only problems he caused were who got to do what for him. We loved him so much.

When I look back at photos of when I was growing up I see a little girl with a smile on her face, loving life and just being happy. Even when I look at pictures of me in elementary, middle, and high school, I see a girl surrounded by a group of friends. I loved school, and through my experiences in elementary, middle, and high school I have become the person that I remain today.

During elementary and middle school, I fell in love with math and science. I loved thinking about how and why things worked. In fourth grade my teacher Mrs. Smith said to my mom, "Abbey is an excellent student with a desire to learn. She may not be able to spell cancer, but she will be able to find a cure for it." That is how I have always been and I believe that is who I will always be.

In addition to academics, I was involved in a number of other activities, including gymnastics, figure skating, rollerblading, volleyball, track and field, and Girl Scouts. I loved being involved in many things, and I loved being surrounded by people. Perhaps this is why depression has changed my life. When you are depressed, at least for me nothing matters. My environment became unimportant as did my relationships with others.

The good old days of childhood are long gone and I don't know where they went. When you fall into depression your life changes in ways you would never even imagine. Everything from your diet to your social life changes. When I look back at my experience with depression, I realized that every aspect of my life as I knew it changed.

I gained 20 pounds in one summer, I was irritated all of time, I was sleeping all of the time, and I was very lonely.

Depression is kind of an ironic thing, you feel extremely lonely, yet you don't want be around anyone. That may sound really odd, but it's true. You wake up and you're sad that you are alone, but to be with other people would take too much energy. It is a vicious cycle of loneliness. It's hard for me to think about the person I was before depression, and the person depression has made me become. I was such a lucky child; I had anything a child could hope for. I had a family that loved me and friends all around me.

I believe that sometimes society tells us that a depressed person comes from an unhappy home, that there is a certain type of family life that can create a depressed person. I believe that this is untrue. I had everything that a child could hope for. I was always supported by my family and friends. I want you to understand that depression can strike anyone, of any age, race, gender, and even people from happy homes.

What Does Depression Feel Like?

Looking back over the last ten months I have had many ups and downs. I suffered from depression for five months before I was willing to accept that I was in fact suffering from depression. It's hard for me to write about my personal experience with depression. Now that I am feeling much better, I would much rather forget what it was like. All throughout my illness I wrote about how I was feeling. I have included one journal entry that I wrote during my battle:

Outwardly you would never know that I suffer from major depression. I present myself to the world as a strong, determined, and compassionate person. If you asked my friends, family, colleagues, or coworkers to describe me they would say something like, "Abbey is a kind, loving, and compassionate person."

I have a lot going on for me in my life. I just got engaged to the love of my life, Mike, after six years of dating him. I am a full time student attending Capital University; and I hold a cumulative grade point average of 3.8 and a 4.0 in my major. I just got accepted into an honors society for all of my academic achievements. In addition I have a great job where I get to work with truly wonderful people. My job involves working with young children. Children bring me joy; I watch them mature and discover the world around them. Overall my life on the outside seems pretty characteristic of a 21 year old. I am a typical college student who loves the academics of college, holds a part time job, and values relationships from both the past and present.

Although I am somehow able to hold everything together when I am in any type of social situation, I have a second and entirely private dimension of my life. Unless you have personally experienced major depression, you would never be able to fully understand how I feel. How sad I am in my dark and lonely world.

So where does my dark world of loneliness come into play? The answer to that question is everyday, all day. If you are around me a lot you will get a glimpse into my dark and lonely world every now and then.

In my everyday life I have two faces I can choose to wear. The face almost everyone around me sees. The one that is hard working, compassionate about life, determined, and so on. The other face I only allow a few people to see. This is a face of undying despair. This face takes no energy to wear because when I wear this face all my true feelings come out. I allow myself to sink lower and lower into my own gloom. There are days when I do not even get out of bed until 5:00pm or 6:00pm, and I will return to bed after I eat dinner, maybe an hour or two later. When I have days like this I truly feel that my dreams are better than anything that I could be faced with in reality. When I am asleep and dreaming I have a chance to escape my own reality. I could equate it with having some kind of terrible physical pain, and knowing a way to make it go away instantly, only to know that as soon as I stop doing whatever it was I was doing to stop the pain, the pain is going to come back just as strong if not stronger. My mental state equates the pain and sleep is how I know that I can make it go away.

I know many other ways to make the pain go away temporally. One way I have learned is that if I am able to keep myself very busy, I do not have enough time to sit and think about how down or alone I feel. I do keep myself very busy during the school weeks. I am a full time student, holding a part time job working three school nights a week. I try to keep good grades, and actively conduct research in the fields of social, personality, and developmental psychology. Although I keep very busy during the school week I allow myself to rest on the weekends. I escape from my depression on the weekends through sleep.

In most of my social interactions, I prefer to wear the first face that I described. I let people see this side of me but it is not easy. Imagine having to act like someone you are not, all of the time. I am not saying that I am not a good, caring, hardworking person; I am saying that I am hardly ever as happy as I lead people to believe. I try to act inline with our society's standards of normal behavior. For example when I am walking around campus I would much rather be invisible because at least then I would not have to smile at all of my acquaintances as I pass them. There are people at my school that I do enjoy seeing; mostly people that I met before I fell into my depression. Such people include my dad, who works at my school, my sister, who attends my school, my professors, and my friends.

As you may be able to guess, it is very hard making new friends; even if I am having a good day and I talk to someone new. It is hard for me to build a relationship with them because I may tell them I will call them later to hang out, but later I may be feeling really down and in turn I will not call them. Through my experience people do not want to make friends with people who do not follow through with their word.

In order to make my life easier I keep the people who knew me and loved me before I was depressed very close. I have told all of these people what I am going through and they are all very supportive of me. I talk to many of them about how I am feeing and they help me work through it. When I am around these people I do not really wear one face over the other. I just really try not bring my friends down with me. Every now and then these people get a glimpse into my world. They will see this look of gloom all over my face, and they will tell me to smile. I will smile for them and every now and then I will feel better briefly. Another common thing that I hear people say who don't even know me is, "Come on now, life is not that bad," perhaps they are trying to make me feel better, but it reminds me of how bad I feel.

When I was depressed I really felt like I was alone. I have always been a quiet person; even a bit shy at times, but depression made it near impossible to talk to others about what I was going through. I did not want to talk about how I was feeling, so I would just write as if I was telling people about my troubles. I could at least express what I was feeling. I was so ashamed about how I was feeling that I did not want to let anyone see me suffer. I would always wear the first face around everyone; that way I would not be confronted by anyone for acting abnormal. Only the people who were around me a lot called me out. If you ever feel like you may be depressed, seek medical attention; please don't hide how you are feeling from others. Let them help you. You can feel much better if only you let others help you.

Falling Over the Edge

It all started when I was a camp counselor. I worked for a summer with poverty stricken children ages six to twelve years old. I saw children go through things that children should never have to go through. I don't really know why this pushed me over the edge. If I had to guess why working with these children led to my depression, I would have to say that the experience was the most stressful experience of my life. I never felt stress so mentally and physically demanding as this.

My campers were between the ages of six and seven years old. Most of the campers were African American and a few were Somolian. As you may or may not know there is some friction between these two different cultures. For the first few weeks of camp I watched six and seven year olds almost get into fist fights daily simply because of cultural differences. One of my campers, Ali, was always teased because he did not understand English very well. "Oh, hell yeah, hell yeah," he was screaming one day. All of my fellow counselors and I just stood there wondering why Ali thought it would be okay to talk like that. At the time he had been running through the sprinkler. We called him aside and spoke with him about how what he was saying was not appropriate. His parents did not speak any English so it turned out that the other campers thought it would be funny to teach him that phrase to get him in trouble.

This behavior continued for several weeks and then one day a remarkable thing happened; Ali and my other campers had become good friends. All of my campers lived in government housing in the same neighborhood. I overheard the children talking about how there was a fight, and when I heard this I went over and asked the kids what happened. "Well Ali was going to get messed up by these other kids, so we got on our bikes and chased them away. Ali is our friend; we can't let him get messed up." I have to say that before this point in time I was never so happy to hear about a fight. My campers learned that they were not so different after all and became good friends.

As a camp counselor I was able to help my campers learn how to build relationships and that was very rewarding for me. On the other hand there were many things that I had to see children go through that I could not do anything about. This was very hard for me to deal with. I saw children come to camp who wore the same clothes several days in a row. In my group of campers I had three, six year old, male triplets. They owned three outfits. The outfits looked like little sports jerseys. They had one blue one, one green one, and one red one. All three boys took turns wearing the different colors.

On other occasions I saw children come to camp that had not been fed since the last time that we fed them, anywhere from one to three days earlier. We would send the children home on Friday with their tummies full and on Monday they would come to us crying because they had not been fed a full meal since we last feed them. I do not believe that the parents were neglecting their children; I do, however, believe that they were simply unable to provide for them.

One day at camp we were all in the bathroom washing our hands before lunch. I turned around and one of the triplets, Tristan was peeing in the toilet. Quickly I made all of the children leave the restroom as did I. During lunch I called Tristan over and asked him, "Tristan why did you go to the bathroom when all of us were in there?" He stared back at me rather confused, as if he did not understand that it was wrong. "Tristan only one person can use the bathroom at a time," I explained to him, "I am going to have to write you up because you went to the bathroom with all of us in there with you." Tristan started crying. He had no idea that it was not okay to use the restroom with all of us there. I later found out that there were at least ten people living in his house and the poor boy never had any privacy at home. He really did not know that he should wait until he was alone to use the restroom.

Another one of my camper's fathers was shot in the head. It was very devastating. How do you help a six year old child fit into a group of his peers for eight hours a day when a child has gone through something like that? As you can imagine working with these children was the hardest, and most rewarding thing that I have ever done. It took a lot out of me.

Six-thirty a.m. I would wake up and carpool to camp. Then all of the counselors would set up for the day. We all did activities throughout the day such as; teambuilding, outdoor classroom, farming, harvesting, eating, hiking, swimming, gym games, and circle time. By 4:30 p.m., I was exhausted and it would be time to carpool home again. I would go home and eat something real quick and go straight to bed. Then around 9:30 p.m., I would get up and go out with my friends only to return several hours later, sleep and go to camp the next morning bright and early.

As you can imagine this was an exhausting schedule, and I went through it Monday through Friday for twelve weeks. During this time I was putting all of my energy into my job. When I was not at work, I just wanted to sleep, and if I had to be up, I was very irritable. I had the idea that after the summer was over I would start feeling much better.

Fortunately, I was able to escape from camp to Florida over the Fourth of July with my soon to be fiancé, and regain some sense of sanity. The vacation was a time of rest, sunshine, and love. Mike proposed to me on July second on the beach at sunset; it was amazing. We felt like two young children in Disney World and in fact the next day we went to all of the theme parks, rode the rides, and watched the shows. It was great. I was very happy to be spending all of this quality time with Mike. On the Fourth of July, we went to the beach and watched the fireworks over the ocean. That is an experience that I will never forget. The way that the fireworks sparkled over the water was hallucinogenic. The vacation was amazing but it had to come to an end all too quickly, and I had to return to the reality of my summer commitment.

I was again exhausted and irritable, but I had hope that it would all go away when camp was over, just as it had when I was in Florida. Before I knew it the summer was over and I had to say goodbye to all of my campers. It was a very bittersweet moment; on one hand I was happy that my commitment was over, and on the other hand I hoped that somebody would take care of my campers.

Several weeks passed where I was able to rest and return to my normal self again. In my mind I thought I was okay after I had rested up for a while; it turns out I was wrong and in denial for along time. Working with disadvantaged children, seeing what they had to go through in combination with the level of stress that I had to face seems to have pushed me over the edge and into depression.

Denial and Acceptance

How could my depression be so obvious to others, and at the same time be so hard for me to comes to terms with? Can we say major denial? In my case I was denying a personal problem as well as my reality. When a person is in denial it takes something to help them realize that they are in fact in denial. In my case it took my fiancé, Mike, to really prove to me that I was in denial. Mike and I met in middle school. He was a friend to me before he became my boyfriend; he always wanted the best for me. Sometimes I think that he knows me better than I know myself. In the eighth grade we started dating and have been together ever since. Mike is my best friend and whenever I need anything he is always there for me. When I became depressed, Mike realized it long before I did.

Mike hinted to me all of the time that there was something different about me and that I should try to get help. I kept telling him that he was crazy, that I was fine and he should stop worrying. However he persistently told me that I needed to seek help. To some this persistence may seem cruel, but looking back I realize that it was necessary. You must understand that at this point in time I had been in a relationship with Mike for over six years. He knows me like he knows himself and he could see that I was sick and that I was not myself.

Five months later, Mike eventually convinced me there was something wrong with me. Now that Mike and I were on the same side our main focus was to get me the help that I so desperately needed; it was time for a game plan.

After I accepted the fact that I needed help, I decided to seek medical attention. This in itself presented a problem. I was a college student still under my parent's health insurance. Since I no longer lived with my parents they were not fully aware of my problem. To find a doctor covered by their plan I decided to tell them about my problems. They were more than willing to listen and help me through this. They sent me to their family doctor; whom they have the utmost respect for.

I was very grateful for all of my parents' support. Even at the age of twenty, my mom still came with me to the doctor's office, and waited for me in the waiting room. I was very happy that she was there because it was at this appointment that I received my first official diagnosis.

I will never forget that doctor's appointment. I sat there anxious and waiting to meet my new doctor whom I wished could alleviate some of my agony. When I finally met him he was not what I had expected. He was a short man in his mid to late fifties. He wore khaki pants, a blue striped shirt, and he finished his look off with a dark blue bowtie. He had a very kind face that reminded me of my grandpa. I had pictured in my mind a much younger, taller, better dressed doctor. But then I realized that it did not matter what he looked like if he could help me.

When he came into my exam room he introduced himself, shook my hand and got down to business. "How have you been feeling lately?" He asked me.

"I just don't really feel like myself lately. I don't really know why I feel different; something just does not feel right."

"How have you been sleeping?" He asked.

"I have been sleeping all night and a majority of my free time during the day."

"How have you been eating?" He asked

"Well I don't really think that I have been eating more or less than normal. I have gained 20 pounds over this summer though."

"I see," he sounded rather concerned. "Do you think that you are depressed?" He asked.

"I think that I could be." I said. After a battery of questions, I heard the words,

"You are suffering from depression." Followed by, "Abbey, why did you wait so long to come and get help?" I really had no good answer that I was willing to admit out loud. I believe the real answer was that I felt ashamed.

To some this official diagnosis may be hard to hear and accept. To me it brought a sense of relief. Something was wrong with me and I was given new hope that something could be done to help me.

After the diagnosis he explained to me what causes depression in most people. "In the brain there are neurons, and these neurons release neurotransmitters. A neurotransmitter is a chemical; and these chemicals float around in the fluid that is in your brain." He continued, "There are receptors for these neurotransmitters. Depression is most commonly due to a chemical imbalance of the neurotransmitter serotonin."

My doctor discussed treatment next. My major is psychology so I had some knowledge of my treatment options. I told my doctor that I was skeptical of medications and I would like to try another route. After about an hour of the history of antidepressant medications and current statistics, he somewhat convinced me that medications were the best option for my treatment. He told me that he thought selective serotonin reuptake inhibitors or SSRI's would be the best option for my treatment. He told me that SSRI's block the reuptake of serotonin and that means that there would be more serotonin floating around in my brain.

"I would like to have you take 20 mg of Prozac daily." He warned, "You may get worse for a week and then after about a month you should start feeling some relief." He also told me that I could expect some weight loss due to a decrease in appetite. "You should feel more awake during the day and be able to sleep well at night." He also requested extensive lab tests to rule out any unknown medical conditions. "I would like to see you back in six weeks."

I took the medication as prescribed for six weeks and went through all of the lab tests. In those six weeks of being on the medication I experienced many different things. Firstly, I experienced major relief from my irritability. For example, if Mike would show up a few minutes late I did not lose it anymore. It seemed like the little things that really upset me before did not even phase me now. I also felt somewhat less sad but I still had down days. I would have days where I would be happy that the sun was shining and I believed that life was good again. I believed that it would be okay to wake up and face the world. I did however have days where I did not want to go out and face the world. Overall I don't think that I really received any great deal of benefits from the medication. I can say that my relationships improved because I was less irritable. I also got a glimpse into my old world.

In addition to the benefits of Prozac, I experienced many side effects. I completely lost my appetite. You know that feeling that you get in your stomach when you are getting hungry, the growling? I lost that. I never craved food; even when I would eat something that I would have previously enjoyed, it would not even taste good. Before Prozac one of my favorite foods was chocolate. After Prozac, I would eat one piece and it just tasted bland. It was not even worth eating. As a result of my loss of appetite, I lost eight pounds in six weeks.

Even worse than losing my appetite was losing my ability to sleep. I would be tired all day long and I would not be able to sleep during the day or at night as I so desperately wanted to do. I would lie awake day and night at least three days in a row every single week. Before Prozac the only sleeping problem I had was wanting to sleep too much.

In addition to losing my appetite and the ability to sleep I developed something quite disturbing. I began having muscle spasms and twitches in my legs and arms. Now I know that many people experience occasional spasms here and twitches there; but mine were occurring at least once every few seconds. "Why are you moving your toe like that?" Mike asked me.

"What are you talking about? I'm not moving my toe." Then I looked down at my big toe and sure enough it was moving.

So after six weeks of some relief and unwanted side effects it was time to go back to the doctors for a follow up.

I returned to the doctors feeling somewhat better but rather concerned about the side effects I had been experiencing. I was called in from the waiting room, with Mike by my side. (My doctor requested that he come with me.) I was asked to step on the scale and sure enough I had lost eight pounds since my last visit. The nurse then led me back into one of the exam rooms, and took my blood pressure and heart rate. She then told me that the doctor would be right with me.

There were two knocks and the doctor entered the exam room. I was a little nervous because I was there for a follow-up as well as hearing the results of my lab report. He went over my lab report first. I learned that my cholesterol was 257 and that I have Beta Thalassaemia Minor, a blood condition from Mediterranean descent where I have a defective production of hemoglobin. Besides those two things I was given a healthy report.

Finally we got into talking about how I felt now that I had been on Prozac for six weeks. I told him that I was a lot less irritable and that overall I felt a little better. To my surprise when I told him about my side effects he seemed rather undaunted. He told me that my side effects were *idiosyncratic,* and that I should not worry about them. This was upsetting because he also told me that he thought I may have to stay on Prozac for the rest of my life. When I heard that I may have to be medicated for the rest of my life, I wanted to make sure that I would have to experience as few side effects a possible.

After talking about my lab report and my medication, my doctor said I would like to check your pulse. I was thinking to myself, your nurse already did that, but I kept my mouth shut. He checked my pulse and looked concerned. He said, "Your heart is beating at 100 beats a minute; it was earlier as well I wanted to check again to see if it slowed down at all." He told me that he would like to do an EKG just to be safe. After the EKG was completed he came back into my exam room and told me that he thought everything was okay. I did not know what to make of what had just happened; I left knowing that I had very high cholesterol for my age and a racing heart. I would later find out that most likely my heart was racing due to anxiety and my high cholesterol is genetic.

Accept Doctor's Advice?

Well Christmas had come and gone and I still didn't feel like my old self. It had been a number of weeks and I had experienced no relief from my side effects. Why should I live perhaps the rest of my life experiencing these side effects? At this point in time I was particularly upset that my doctor had not listened to what I had been saying about the side effects I had been experiencing. It almost felt as if this doctor didn't care about how I felt. I can deal with one or two sleepless nights, but to miss three nights of sleep every week was very upsetting and hard to deal with.

In addition to feeling like my doctor had not been listening to me and my personal concerns about my health, I was even more disturbed when my mom came home from her doctor's appointment. My mom had gone in for simple blood tests. She came home on Prozac. "What did you talk with the doctor about?" I asked her.

"I told him how I liked cleaning a lot and that sometimes I get anxious about how the house looks." She told me. (Now keep in mind there three kids in our house, a dog, and my dad, who is a landscaper. Our house does need cleaned daily to keep up with all the traffic in and out.) Come to find out our family doctor told my mom that she was suffering from of obsessive compulsive disorder (OCD). He told her that the medication may not make her feel that much better but it will make the lives of the people who live with her easier. What a slap in the face, why would a doctor say something like that?

I have lived with my mom for most of my life, and I honestly don't think that she has obsessive compulsive disorder. Yes, she likes things clean, but it doesn't affect her everyday life. She still functions, she is still able to cook dinner, go to work, and so on. So she likes having a clean house, what's wrong with that? I like living in a clean house, does that mean that I have this disorder too? According to our doctor anyone who has a clean house is suffering from obsessive-compulsive disorder.

Anyways after my mom came home on Prozac, I really started to question my doctor's diagnosis and advice. I came to the conclusion that my doctor really liked Prozac. One time when I was in his office he was telling me how he's put hundreds of people on Prozac, and that it was a great drug. After a lot of thought I decided to go get another opinion.

I decided that I was going to go talk with Dr. Torello, a psychologist at my university. Dr. Torello is my academic adviser as well as one of my professors. I have the utmost respect for him; whenever I need somebody to talk to about school or things that are going on in my life he's always there to listen.

It was on a Wednesday afternoon when I met with Dr. Torello to discuss what had been going on in my life. "How have you been?" he asked me.

"I've been okay." I said and continued, "I was diagnosed with depression recently and have been depressed for nearly seven months." Dr. Torello looked surprised to learn that I was depressed. Dr. Torello is one of those people who I did not want to let down. I always tried to have a smile on my face around him. He is a great person and he tends to take things personally, if you don't smile at him or laugh at him, he will think he did something to offend you and he'll keep apologizing. I didn't want him to take the way that I was acting personally, so I always tried to be happy around him.

He asked me about some of my symptoms. "How long have you been feeling this way?"

"I think that it started when I was a camp counselor this summer. I had a really hard time seeing what some children have to endure. I thought that after camp was over I would be my old self again. That did not seem to happen."

Dr. Torello then asked me, "I know that you are a very sensitive person, do you think that maybe you feel down because of your experience with these kids and maybe you're not depressed?"

"I suppose it could be that."

I told Dr. Torello that I was depressed but that I was concerned with how my doctor was choosing to treat me. I explained to him how I was having side effects and my doctor didn't think it was a big deal. I also told him how my mom came home on Prozac and was diagnosed with OCD. Dr. Torello asked me what I had been prescribed, and I told him 20 mg of Prozac daily. Then he gave me his advice; "I think that it may be a good idea to go and see a psychiatrist. He can give you a full evaluation and find out what may be wrong." He explained to me how a psychiatrist is more specialized in this area and that he would be better able to treat me. He gave me the name of a psychiatrist, and then he helped me contact my medical insurance company to see if this doctor was covered under my plan. The doctor was, so it was now up to me to make the appointment.

I thanked Dr. Torello for his time and his patience with me; and then I headed back to my room to make the phone call. I picked up my phone and dialed the seven numbers that would change my life. The phone rang three times and then a woman answered the line. This woman was very soft-spoken, her voice was so soothing that for a moment I wondered if she was real. She asked me what the nature of my phone call was, I told her I had been diagnosed with depression and I was being treated but that I was having bad side effects. She asked me two questions, "Do you ever have thoughts about killing yourself? Do you ever think about harming others?" Fortunately I was able to answer no to both of these questions. After answering these questions I was able to schedule my appointment; it was set for the following Friday.

I received a phone call a week early and was notified that they had an opening at 2:30 p.m. I told them that I would be able to make it.

That same day I had scheduled lunch with my great Aunt Edie at 11:30 a.m. I went out to lunch with her and we reminisced about her life. She told me stories about the Great Depression, and about her life in Washington, DC. She told me stories about my dad growing up, and stories about my grandpa and my grandma. Then I told her about my college life academically and socially, and before I knew it we were talking about my depression and the doctor's appointment that I had to go to later that afternoon. It was at that point in time when I realized that I was a bit frightened. I didn't really understand why I was frightened; I think it was because I was going to see a psychiatrist. I think the whole social stigma of having a psychiatrist was getting to me. Aunt Edie told me not to worry I would be all right. After hearing her say that I calmed down quite a bit.

Meeting My Psychiatrist

Two-thirty p.m. rolled around and it was time to meet my psychiatrist. His office was about a half-hour away from where I lived so I made sure I was on the road by 1:45 p.m. I knew that I would have to fill out paperwork when I arrived. Around 2:15 p.m. I reached my destination.

Surprisingly the building looked just as I imagined it. It was a two-story brick building with four white columns holding up the balcony. I took a deep breath and got out of my car. Slowly I walked towards the building. To my surprise the inside of the building was very inviting. At both ends of the foyer there were two spiral staircases heading downstairs. I walked down the stairs and found the suite were I would meet my new psychiatrist, Dr. Moore.

I opened the door and walked in; there was no one to be seen. There was a small waiting room and to my right there was an office. Straight ahead there was a set of double doors. I couldn't see what was beyond that. I decided to walk into the office on my right and sure enough there was the woman whose voice I heard on the phone. She gave me a clip board with a stack of papers on it that I had to fill out. I took the clipboard and went back into the waiting room. As I was filling out the papers a curly haired man walked into the room and proceeded through the double doors.

That curly haired man turned out to be my psychiatrist. Several minutes had passed when he came out to the waiting room and asked me to follow him. I'm not sure what to call the room that I followed him into; it was kind of like an exam room and an office. There was a desk and two chairs, a couch, and two armchairs. He shook my hand, and introduced himself, "Hi Abbey, I'm Dr. Moore." He was tall, had blond curly hair and wore glasses. He put me at ease right away by inviting me to sit wherever I felt comfortable. I choose to take a seat on the couch and he sat in the armchair adjacent to me.

He started our conversation out by asking what had been going on. I told him, how I saw a doctor and that I was diagnosed with depression. "I am having lots of side effects and my doctor didn't seem to listen to me. I was almost willing to accept what my other doctor had told me, until my mom came home on Prozac and was diagnosed with OCD. I think that my doctor may like Prozac a little too much."

After he gained a better understanding of why I was there he began asking me questions. He asked me about my sleeping habits, my mood, my relationships, my side effects, extra stress I might have in my life, and he also asked me about my family history. We talked about the different reasons that I might be tired, my relationships, and how I felt about my side effects.

One thing that was very different about Dr. Moore versus the other doctor that I had seen was that he *really* listened to what I was saying. He knew how to get me to open up and tell him things that I have never told anyone. After we talked for about an hour he asked, "Well do you want to know what I think?" Of course I said yes, and he told me, "When I first saw you in the waiting room I could tell what was wrong with you. I do think that you are depressed, but on top of that you looked rather sedated. I think that you are overdosed on Prozac."

An overdose on Prozac? I had never heard of such a thing. My other doctor told me that even if somebody was not depressed and they took Prozac it would not affect them in any way. So I never thought that I could be overdosed. My psychiatrist explained to me that most of the side effects I was experiencing were due to an overdose. When I heard that, I was very happy that I decided to seek a second opinion. I could not believe that my other doctor never said anything to me about an overdose. If I had not sought a second opinion, I would still be living with the side effects that I had been experiencing.

So how could I be treated and get rid of these side effects was the next question. My doctor decided to cut my dosage in half. I was taking 20 mg of Prozac daily; so I was supposed to take 10 mg of Prozac daily now. My doctor told me that my blood level would change as a result from changing from 20 mg to 10 mg over the course of about a week or two. He told me that I should call him if I started feeling worse instead of better.

After he wrote my prescription, I entered the office to pay and make my next appointment. He wanted to see me back in two weeks. With an overwhelming feeling of relief I left his suite, and went outside to my car. On the way to the pharmacy I called my mom to tell her the good news; I was going to feel better and with any luck my side effects would be gone.

A few days had passed and I started feeling a lot better. Music sounded very different to me. It reached me at a level I forgot existed. I was really shocked at how great I was feeling. Then something very curious happened, I started feeling really down, worse than I felt before. I called Dr. Moore and told him how I had been feeling and he decided to change my dosage to 15mg of Prozac instead of 10mg. He had warned me that this might happen, and then he reminded me that I had an appointment with him in several days and we could talk more about how I was feeling then.

The Good News

Well six days came and passed and it was time to go back and see my psychiatrist again. The drive to his office was the same except instead of being nervous this time I was very excited. I could not wait to tell Dr. Moore how much better I was doing. I was still having a hard time believing that I was actually doing this much better; however it had been several days and I still was feeling great.

As I approached the same two-story brick building, I walked up to the doors, this time with a new bounce in my step. I entered the building, walked down the spiral staircase, and found Dr. Moore's suite. When I entered his suite to my surprise everything looked the same; but somehow it also looked different. I could not really put my finger on what felt different until I really started to look at my surroundings. I sat down on the couch and I waited to be called back. As I was sitting there I noticed what was different, I realized that it was not the office that was different, it was me. I was beginning to notice the beauty in life again. You know how it feels when you get a new eye glasses prescription? Everything looks the same as it did before, but somehow it looks so much richer and more detailed. That's kind of how I felt. I was able to see beauty again.

The first time that I was in Dr. Moore's office all that I noticed was the general lay out of the suite. This time however I noticed the fine details of the office. Instead of sitting on the couch looking at the floor, I noticed that there were pictures hanging on the wall in front of me. The pictures were of beautiful nature scenes. Below the pictures there was a bookshelf filled with all types of books and magazines. How could I not have noticed this the first time that I was there? I was truly looking past a whole dimension of my life that was right in front of me.

Then, before I could sit and think about all the things that I had missed in the décor of Dr. Moore's office, he stepped out of his room and called me back. I again sat on the couch and he sat in the armchair adjacent to me. Dr. Moore said that I looked much less sedated than I did the last time that he saw me. We talked about how I was feeling, my side effects, and my relationships. I described to him how music sounded different to me and how I was noticing things in my everyday surroundings that I had not noticed before. He said, "It sounds as if you are able to stop and smell the roses again." I thought about what he had said for a moment and then I discovered, that this was in fact what was different in my life, I was able to stop and smell the roses again.

After we had this breakthrough, we discussed my next visit. Dr. Moore informed me that when the seasons change we may have to change my dosage again because of the effects of natural light on serotonin levels. He asked me to come back in the early spring so we could again evaluate my situation. In addition to all of this good news, Dr. Moore told me that he would like to try and take me off of Prozac in the summer and see how I respond. I was very excited to hear this, because when I was first diagnosed I was told that Prozac could be a life long medication for me. I have decided that even if I do find out that I need to stay on Prozac after I go off of it, at least I'll know that I tried.

Control

Most people think that a depressed person will hurt themselves or attempt suicide in the deepest parts of depression. This is not true. In fact suicide attempts occur most often when falling in or out of depression. When a person is in the deepest depths of depression they may contemplate suicide, but they simply don't want to waste the time and energy in planning and carrying out the suicide. In contrast, when a person is falling in or out of depression, they are still feeling bad, but they have the necessary energy for planning and attempting suicide.

I had been on the correct dosage of Prozac for about three weeks; when I did something that I still have a hard time believing. Mike came over and we got in a fight about him supporting me. After Mike went home that night, I took a shower to try and calm myself down. I thought that I may be okay if I could just relax. I was in the shower for about 20 minutes and I was no calmer when the shower was over. I needed to do something to take the pain away.

Then for the first time I was unable to resist the urge to do something to myself that I never thought I would ever be able to do. I took a needle out of a box. I got out a lighter and I sterilized the tip of the needle. I sat down in my black chair and rolled up my shorts. Then I put the tip of the needle to my skin and I started to scrape my skin off layer, by layer. It was a slow and painful way of relieving my mental pain. I was now in control. I hate losing control of myself, and now I found a way that I could be in control of my pain. I kept scraping, there was one line of skin missing and bleeding. One line no longer seemed to be enough; I slowly created a second line. Two lines were not enough, I created a third. I looked down and I was pleased. I was in control again.

The next morning I picked up the phone and I called Mike. The phone began to ring, "Hello" Mike answered.

"Hi" then I paused, "I need to tell you something."

"What is wrong?" Mike asked me.

"I did something last night after you left."

"What did you do?" He asked, now sounding rather concerned.

"I hurt myself." There was silence.

"How did you hurt yourself?" "Did you cut yourself?" He asked.

"Yes" I answered him after a long pause. I knew that I would have to explain to him sooner or later why there were three fresh cuts on the top of my thigh so when he asked how I hurt myself I told him.

"Why did you do that?" Mike asked me. "Why would you hurt yourself?"

"I did not know what to do and I was hurting. It seemed like a good idea at the time," I answered him. The conversation went on for a while; neither of us knowing what to say or think.

Throughout my entire experience with depression, I never thought about attempting suicide. I have to admit that I did think about suicide a lot, but I never thought about it as an option for myself. I thought about how much easier it would be to just end it all; but I have to say that I fear God too much to ever end my own life. I just kept trying to tell myself that everything had to get better.

After I began coming out of depression, I did not really think about suicide as much as I thought about it when I was falling into depression. I thought about ways of controlling my own pain, and when I was tempted, I decided to take control. After I took action, I felt immediate satisfaction. After some time passed all I felt was a sense of shame. As the cuts were healing I received a constant reminder of what I had done. Every night when I was trying to fall asleep I would roll over onto the cuts and feel the pain of what I had done to myself. Every time I change my cloths, even today I have to see the scars. In a way I am glad that I have the scars, because it is a constant reminder of what I have done.

I think that it is very important for anyone affected by depression to understand that even if a person seems to be doing better, they are not out of the woods. I really thought that I was doing better when I hurt myself but when it comes down to it, I still need to learn how to cope with disappointment. I have decided to keep a journal about this so that you can go through this experience with me.

Help Me!

The first time that I cut myself I was looking for a way of taking away the pain but in addition to this, I knew by hurting myself I would be hurting Mike, and this would be a way of manipulating him. After I hurt myself I thought that I would never do it again but, recently when I am faced with a stressful and upsetting situation, I always think about cutting. The only thing that stops me is the fact that if Mike sees anymore cuts on me, he will be very disappointed. I know that something is not right; I should not be having these thoughts. Up until now the only person who I have told about my cutting is Mike. I am very ashamed of what I have done to myself, but for some reason, it still feels like a reasonable option, and not as a means of manipulation, but rather control of my mental pain. I have decided to call Dr. Moore and tell him what I have done. I hope that he can help me come up with an affective coping strategy.

Not Again

I have always been a very ambitious person. Since I have been on Prozac I have experienced a decreased drive to succeed. At first I perceived this as a very good thing. I felt much more relaxed. I stopped worrying about being so perfect in my school work. Now however I am beginning to realize that I need to keep up the trend that I have created for myself, as far as grades go. I am used to receiving all A's in my major, and I am now experiencing a difficult time keeping a B average in several courses. I think that Prozac may be to blame for my decreased drive to succeed and this is a major concern of mine. I am trying to get into graduate school next year and I need near perfect grades to get into the schools of my choice.

Today all I could think about was cutting; I was upset about my most recent lack of achievement in school. I decided to go to work like usual, because I thought that it may take my mind off of cutting, and it did. When I got off work I had dinner, and then when I was in my room, I was reminded of my troubles in school. I took a shower and I tried to think about my other options, I turned the water on really hot so that I would only be able to think about that. Turns out the water could not get hot enough. Then I tried to do some breathing exercises and that did not work either. Finally I decided to look down at my body and find a place where I could cut where no one would notice. I considered in between my toes, in between the joints on my toes, and then I looked at my watch. I thought that I could cut around my wrist and I would be able to cover it up with my watch. When I got out of the shower I decided to cut again; this time with a razor. I decided to cut underneath my watch.

After I cut again, I realized that I was really in trouble. I realized that cutting may really become a problem. I started thinking that I really wanted to cut and I began to think that it works. I know that it is wrong, but I can't help thinking about it. I have decided to make an appointment with Dr. Moore. I believe that if I tell him what I have done, he will try to talk me out of it and convince me not to do it any more. I hope more than anything that he will at least hold me accountable for my actions.

The Call

I cut for the second time yesterday; and I have decided to make an appointment with Dr. Moore. I called and he is able to see me in a few days. I am really nervous about talking with him about this, but I know that it is for the best. I need to tell someone what I have done. I hope that he will help me stop.

The Visit

It is the first day of spring and today I went to see Dr. Moore; we had a lot to talk about. I wanted to talk to him about my cutting as well as my decreased ambition in my school work. When I arrived I was very nervous about telling him that I began cutting; his office was playing classical music which really helped me relax. He came out of the consultation room and greeted me with a smile. This also helped me relax.

He began our conversation by asking all of the normal questions: how have you been sleeping, eating, feeling…? I told Dr. Moore that I was feeling okay, that I wanted to sleep all of the time again, and that I felt like I was losing ambition in school. He suggested that due to the increased amount of sunlight in the day, that my medication was at too high of a dosage and that I needed to lower my dosage again. He explained that sometimes when the days become longer; it is like you are getting a double dose of medicine, because exposure to sunlight can increase the levels of serotonin in the brain. He suggested that I go from 15 mg daily to only 10 mg daily. Then he told me that come summer time, due to even more sunlight, I should be able to go off of Prozac altogether. I was very excited to hear that there was a chance to be normal again without the aid of medication.

I could have left right then and there, Dr. Moore had already changed my medication and as far as he knew that's all I was there for, but I had to tell him. I needed to be held accountable for my actions. Then I told him about how I had cut myself twice and I was afraid that it might become a habit because it works so well. He told me that cutting is very common and that it does help people feel better because it causes the body to release endorphins. This kind of surprised me, but it makes sense, that I would feel better after I cut because of endorphins.

He told me that I should be concerned because it could become addictive and it is harmful to the body. One thing that kind of surprised me was that he really did not try to talk me out of doing it. I'm just glad that he knows because I know that he will ask me about it in the future and I want to be able to tell him that I no longer cut.

In addition to our discussion of my cutting, Dr. Moore wanted to talk with me about what was going on in a different domain. Dr. Moore knows that I study psychology and he asked me a rather curious question, he asked me if I thought that I had a personality disorder. I was surprised with this question, but knew what he was getting at. He was suggesting that I had Borderline Personality Disorder or BPD. I said no and he left it at that. Although I said no at the time, I think that it is a possibility. BPD can be characterized by fear of real or imagined abandonment, and a blend of personality and mood disorders sometimes involving self injury. That pretty much defines me, and I would be curious to read my chart and see his notes on this topic. I think at the time I said no because I really only wanted to deal with one mental disorder at a time; denial is a forte of mine.

BPD or not, I cannot stress the importance of keeping a close eye on a depressed person as they are recovering. When I was depressed, I just did not deal with things, I did not feel. When something would be stressful, I would not deal with it, I would go to sleep. I did not have the energy to think about my problems let alone try and deal with them. When I was recovering from depression, I felt like I was on top of the world for awhile. When I realized that I no longer needed to hide from the world, and my reality, I had to figure out a way to adjust to something that I did not have to deal with for a long time. I needed to figure out how to integrate my life back with society. This was a very difficult thing for me to do, and at times I had a hard time learning how to cope. At first I dealt with my troubles by cutting. I am so thankful I realized that I was coping in an unhealthy way. I sought help, and now I am doing much better. I have to be completely honest and say that I still think about cutting, and sometimes I do but, I try just about anything and everything that I can think of before I harm myself. I have found that if I go to the gym, it relieves the stress and instead of releasing endorphins by hurting myself I can feel better in a much healthier way. In addition to working out, pampering myself really seems to help. Sitting down and drinking hot coco, or wrapping myself up in an aromatherapy blanket helps relax me.

When I first started cutting, I was very ashamed about what I was doing and I still am. Everyone knows that it is wrong to inflict harm against oneself. If you accidentally touch something hot you automatically pull your arm away. That's how we are, we try to avoid pain, it's built into us. To harm oneself is unnatural. What most people don't understand is that when someone self injurers they actually feel better, the body produces endorphins, which is kind of like morphine. It takes pain away.

When I went to talk with Dr. Moore, he told me that cutting was common, and that was all that he really said about it. Later, I found out that it is common, even Princess Diana cut herself. It is my hope that society does not shun self injurers, and does not look at them as freaks. I have heard that one too many times. Yes, cutting is a Taboo topic. Many of my friends and family members don't even know that I have ever hurt myself, and I hope that they think no differently of me after they read this. I was almost tempted to leave this part of my story out of this book until I realized that my experience with cutting is an important part of my experience with depression, and that sometimes depression can lead to other potentially dangerous problems such as self injury.

The Follow Up

In mid May I returned to see Dr. Moore for a follow up. For the first part of May my muscles spasms had returned and I was sleeping again all of the time. This was of obvious concern for me. When I told Dr. Moore about all of this, he smiled and said "I think that it is time for you to go off of Prozac, but just to be safe I would like to lower you to 5 mg a day, and then on June 1st, no more Prozac."

This was very exciting news for me, again the dosage of Prozac that I had been taking was too much in combination with the days lengthening and my body no longer needing Prozac. Then Dr. Moore said, "I just want you to know that your depression could return in one year, ten years, next fall, or never; so keep your eyes open for it." Knowing that I had kept myself untreated for five months during my first bout with depression, he wanted to make me well aware that my depression could return and to make sure I would do something about it.

This was the first time I had been to Dr. Moore's office when I did not need to reschedule; and this was very exciting for me. To think I may be *normal* again without the aid of medication to correct a chemical imbalance. When I think about that, I can't help but think that my depression may come back, but if it does I have decided that I can deal with it. I now understand that I am not alone, and that there are a lot of people willing to help me. If you or a loved one is depressed I hope that you realize that there are a lot of people who are willing to help you and there are equally as many people who understand what you are going through; you are not alone.

My Life Now

Eleven months have passed since I fell into my depression. I have learned a lot about myself and the people around me through this experience. I am one of those people who believe that everything happens for a reason. I think that I became depressed for a number of reasons. I believe that I was supposed to understand what depression is all about, and that I am supposed to share my story with others and provide a sense of hope for all of those who are suffering or know someone who is suffering from depression. I also think that since I am a student studying psychology, I was supposed to experience depression so that I would have a great deal of empathy for its sufferers. I am one of those people who thought that depression was a fake illness; I always thought that depressed persons could get over their depression if they just tried hard enough. After experiencing depression first hand I now realize that depression is not something that one can just shake off, but that it is a very real illness.

I have also learned through my illness that there is light at the end of all of the darkness. Slowly I am returning to my *normal* life. I am wanting more and more to be around people. I am able to, as Dr. Moore said, "Stop and smell the roses." It is hard to imagine how different life can be when you suffer from depression. It is the difference between watching color and black and white television. It's the difference between sleeping and facing the world. The music of my life has a completely different tone.

I am really enjoying my life again. I have developed affective coping strategies, that help me resist the urge to cut, and hopefully these strategies will also help me in the future in dealing with possible triggers for another depressive episode. I look forward to going to school and work. I enjoy spending time with my friends and family. My relationship with Mike is back to normal again. When I have a smile on my face it is for real.

However, even though I am feeling well now, I am still continuing treatment and seeing my psychiatrist. I know that it is important to continue treatment, talk about my feelings, and surround myself with supportive people. It is so important to have a supportive team surrounding me in case I fall again.

I would like to add that although I am feeling much more like my old self again; I still have bad days. For those who may be reading this because they are affected by depression in some way, remember this, treatment is just that. It is not a cure, it is not a one hundred percent answer to all of depressions problems; it is simply a treatment.

Through the use of medication I was able to get back to my life. I went into this whole thing against medications, but it is through a combination of a great support system and medications that I am able to be my normal self again.

PART II
My Relationships

Depression and Relationships

According to the *National Institute of Mental Health (2002),* "Depressive illnesses often interfere with the normal functioning and cause pain and suffering not only to those who have a disorder, but also those who care about them. Serious depression can destroy family life as well as the life of the ill person." I believe that it is very important not only to understand how depression affects the person suffering, but also how it affects all of the people around the sufferer.

After learning about how I felt physically and mentally in my lowest points I would like to give the person closest to me a chance to tell how my depression affected him as an individual as well as our relationship.

The number one person besides myself that my depression affected is my fiancé. It should come as no surprise that the one person that I am closest to was affected the most. Once I fell into depression every aspect of our relationship changed. Everything from our phone conversations to our most intimate moments changed.

I asked Mike a series of questions about how my depression affected him as an individual and as my partner. Mike had a very hard time answering some of these questions, although he reluctantly did. I think that he was worried about hurting my feelings, but I told him to be honest and he was.

Describe me when we first started dating.
You were happy, fun to be around, and had a positive outlook in life.
What was going on in my life when I fell into my depression?
You fell into depression when you were a camp counselor. I told you, you should never take that job because I did not think that it was a good job for you.
Describe my personality shortly after you noticed a change in my behavior.
You were very dreary and gloomy; it was hard to see you like that.
Describe our relationship when I was in the lowest point of depression.
You made my life miserable; I hated being around you, you were either asleep, irritable, crying, or upset.

As you can imagine after reading what Mike had to say, our relationship suffered greatly because of my depression. Anything that Mike did I had something to say about it. Whether he did not get over to my house quick enough or he took too long to put his shoes on, I would lose it. I lost it all of the time over nothing. Honestly I do not know how he stayed around to support me through all of this. Mike kept telling me to get help, but I was in denial.

Mike did not show me how much he was struggling with me on the inside; he just bottled it up and helped me though everything. He would even try to comfort me by giving me a hug when he knew I was having a bad day. Of course I was so irritable that the hug only meant that I was a piece of meat that he wanted. This created problems, and I asked Mike to stop showing me any type of physical affection. I told him that if I wanted a hug I would hug him. Mike respected my wishes, and over time I came to realize that he was really trying to comfort me. That helped our relationship a little, but it was not until five months later that Mike convinced me to seek medical attention.

I know that my depression has affected Mike as an individual and as my partner. Below are several questions that I asked Mike to help you understand how depression can affect not only the individual suffering, but their significant others as well.

How did you feel when you found out that I was clinically depressed?
I felt a sense of relief because I knew that something was wrong with you and that you were going to receive the medical attention that you needed.

How did my depression affect our relationship?
Your depression definitely created friction in the beginning because I did not understand what was going on. When I would come over to see you, you were always asleep and if you were awake you were never happy.

Do you worry about my depression affecting our future?
Yes, I do worry a little bit. I worry that a relapse may cause problems between us.

Has my depression affected your mood?
I would not say that I feel depressed, but when you are having a hard time I do feel blue.

Give me a list of adjectives that you have felt through the course of my depression.
Anxious, worried, frustrated, annoyed, neglected, discouraged, and blue.

Describe what you think depression is like.
I can not imagine what it is like; but I think that it could be like having your life shrouded in darkness.

Write about our relationship before, during and after depression.
When I started dating Abbey, we were only fourteen years old and she was relatively happy. She seemed like any other teenage girl, but was fun to be around and had a positive outlook on life. There were no major problems with Abbey, except the expected ones with a teenage girl, but these mattered little to me since I was a teenage guy. I suppose it might be easy for a teenage girl to fall into depression for the simple reason that girls are so mean to each other. Though this may be the case,

Abbey never fell into such a trap that some young adolescents often fall into.

Many who know Abbey and I, have seen that we have been together for quite some time. These first few years were filled with activities that normal adolescents engage in. We would go to the movies with our friends, hang out at friends houses, have dinner together, go to dances, and even in some cases work together. One can see that these kinds of things can at least constitute the makings of an ordinary adolescent. For the most part, Abbey would have a good time at these types of functions. I was certainly having a good time at these types of social gatherings, and I was more than glad to have her around. It was good to be dating a girl that I could have a good time with all the time.

I continued dating Abbey through high school, as we got older we still did the same things that high school kids do. There was nothing out of the ordinary that would happen during this time, although many might contend that is was strange for two young people to be dating for such an extended time. There was nothing wrong with it to us though since we were both happy with things. Looking back that far, there still did not seem to be any depression coming on at that time, which is a vulnerable stage for many as it is. High school seemed to be no big deal to both of us. It was a pretty good time overall, but almost a waist besides social functions and sports. The important thing is that it did not cause any major problems besides the general vexations of high school.

Once we were in college, things stayed relatively the same between us. I had some friends go to colleges elsewhere, but most still stayed in Ohio. Abbey's close friends remained around here too. Besides people moving, there was no big change to either of us. I still see my friends and she does too. Abbey adjusted well to the academic part of school pretty well, but Abbey was not exactly the social butterfly. It was not that big of a deal at first, but later on it would get even worse until she would not want to do much at all.

The first time I actually noticed anything I would actually see as depression was in the summer after Abbey's second year of college. We were both working a lot of hours, but she decided to do a pretty demanding camp counseling job. I warned her of this counseling job and even had a feeling it would be very stressful on her because I know her, but it was a good way to get plenty of hours and even paid more then what she was currently making. I was even personally asked to take this job and turned them down, mostly because of how early it would start in the morning. In any case, Abbey often became irritable and no matter what I said or did, it would remain that way. She would often sleep long hours after work and when I would come over to see her later at night she might still want to sleep and not get out of bed. I would often get very angry about this and told her that it was that job. She agreed that this was a problem, but I believed it had to be more than just that. She seriously had a problem and I got sick of trying to be nice about everything. I told her she should go get help, but she would not listen to me.

This irritability, constant sleeping and other problems occurred throughout the summer. I would often times go to friends by myself since she was just too tired and not in the mood to see anyone. This was all a constant annoyance to me, and it would even put me in a bad mood at times. No matter what I told her, she would not listen at all. I would say that she was gloomy, or dreary, but to her that was just an insult, but what I was saying is that she needed help. We would have our arguments and we were both pretty unhappy. Although she did not realize she was depressed, I was sick and tried of it all, but there were still some good times. We went to Florida where we got engaged and had a good time. This seemed to alleviate some of her immediate stress, but it did not last very long when we got home. The rest of the summer pretty much shaped the same way the earlier part did. She was glad to be engaged, but still irritable and tired. It would be months until she would finally do something about it.

Once Abbey finally believed that she had a problem, she saw a doctor and got on medicine for depression. Things have slowly gotten a little better over the months. She is more like herself now, and there is chance that it will get even better from here. I am guessing that she will continue to get even better, but I am not certain if she will need to continue taking medicine for the depression. I am grateful that things have gotten better for her and I. It is easier to have a good time around her just like we used to and the depression will not affect things like school, work, or other things as long as she is treated and it works. No one wants to be depressed and was important for Abbey and is important for others to get help.

Other Relationships

I was able to hide my depression from many people for a long time. I was able to do this because at the time I was living in a house by myself. The only person who truly knew what I was going through was Mike. He had a key to my place, so he would come over to see me. I was always asleep when he would come over; it did not matter what time of day it was. If it was not for Mike I might not have even gotten out of bed some days.

Although my depression has affected my relationship with my fiancé, Mike, it has also affected many other relationships in my life. There are several groups of people that have been affected, including, my friends and family.

My family really had no idea of what I was going through because I tried to hide it from them. If I was feeling bad I would not answer the phone when they called and when I would see them face to face I would put on my brave face and fake my way through being happy. I was sure that I was only going through a phase and I did not want to worry them. I was sure that I would grow out of this at anytime. When I finally stopped denying that I had a real problem I decided to tell them that I had not been feeling like myself. I told them that I was tired all of the time and that I felt sad for no reason. They were concerned about my health and they wanted me to go get medical attention. They helped me through everything.

When I told my mom that I wanted to write a book about what I had gone through and how it affected the people around me, she thought that it would be a good idea to talk about how I was as a child and how I changed over time; the idea of what normal is for me. In explaining how I was, you are better able to understand how I became different during depression. In addition, you will get to see how I was able to keep my depression from my family, how they felt about that, and finally, what they did to support me.

Abbey was born on January 12, 1985. A beautiful blonde baby girl, such a beautiful pink color. Everyone remarked how pretty she was. I knew Abbey's personality before she was ever born. She was very active moving around inside me, very anxious to born. And she was born two weeks early, raring to go. She has always been very inquisitive. Even as a six month old baby she would recognize that something in her room was out of place or different. I would carry her all around and show her things and tell her what it was; so when she noticed something different, she would point to it right away. She talked at a very early age and very clear, easy to understand. We nicknamed her "Gabby Abbey". She always had something to tell you. She was always very bright and quite a leader. She usually made her own rules to games she played with her sister. Her sister Kaylee came along when Abbey was 19 months old; the two never knew jealousy. She was too young to realize anything. The girls were very close growing up; they did everything together. I was a stay home mom at the time and loved staying home with my children. Her brother Jordy was born in seven years later.

Abbey always did well in school and took her schooling seriously. She always wanted to do well. She was involved in Brownies and Girl Scouts, dance and gymnastics. She loved playing volleyball. She had a great group of friends who remained close all through high school. As Abbey got older, I noticed her compassion for other people. She was more of a serious person who tried to solve everyone's problems. She took religion very seriously; she wasn't one to go out partying, there are more important things in life.

When she turned 14 years old, Abbey went out and got her first job at Kroger's. She works very hard for everything she has; there is not a lazy bone in her body. She's very motivated and whatever she decides to put her mind to, she will complete. Her mind is like a sponge; she can't get enough information. She likes keeping her mind busy, always has. Abbey met Mike when she was in the eighth grade. The two hit it off, and are still together today, as a matter of fact they are engaged. Mike is like another son to us; it feels like he's always been a member of our family.

Abbey graduated from high school and went off to college; things were going great for the first two years. She was so happy. She got a job at a local community center, which eventually led to her being a camp counselor. That's when her troubles started. She worked with disadvantaged children. She cared for these children so much, and worried about them over the weekend's, wondering if they were hungry. If she had them all week she knew they were fine, send them away for a couple days and she worried, that's the seriousness and compassion I see in Abbey. It's wonderful to be that way, but it started to bring her down. I didn't know this was happening until the day Abbey came to me right before she decided to go to the doctors.

I was surprised when she told me she just didn't feel right. I wanted to help her and support her all I could. Now that we know what is going on, it should not have surprised me. I can understand how someone so compassionate could fall into a slump over seeing these children everyday, and worrying about them. Then the end of the summer comes along and she has to say goodbye. She doesn't know if these kids are going to be okay. That's my Abbey, she's going to worry. I had no idea Abbey was going through all this. She hid it very well. When I saw her she seemed fine. She had always been on the serious side, I had no idea she was depressed. Abbey did not live at home, she rented a house, and her roommate moved out, Abbey was living alone. I know she remarked she didn't like being alone, but she liked being independent. I'm so glad that Mike was around, encouraging her to get help. I'm not sure where she'd be today if he hadn't pushed her along. I talked to Abbey almost everyday, and I would see her a couple times a week, but I still had no idea.

You just want the best for your kids; and you want to help them and support them. I feel bad that of all the people, her own mother and father didn't know. We've always been a very close and open family. Abbey knows we love her no matter what, and will be there for her no matter what. I'm so glad that she finally came to me and told me so I could try to get some help for her. She is finally feeling much better; things are coming around for her again. She is surrounded by people who care deeply for her, and we'll all make sure she doesn't slip through the cracks again; and if she does her family and friends will be there to help her.

If you feel depressed and this all sounds too familiar tell someone; don't suffer in silence. You only have one chance on this earth, don't waste your life away, do something about it, get help. Someone does care. You can feel better.

In addition to my family, my friends were also affected by my depression. Again it was not very difficult to hide my depression from them. One of my best friends, Olga, was in a new relationship and was spending a lot of her time with her boyfriend. Another close friend Katie had just started an internship that demanded a lot of her time. So I was not around them a whole lot when I was going through the deepest part of my depression. Again I would only answer my phone when I felt like it, which was not often. When I finally told them what I had been going through they looked very surprised. I have known Olga for eleven years and Katie for seven years and they could not understand what I was talking about. They looked at me with disbelief, I don't know if they were trying to be nice by acting like I could never have a mental disorder, or they really had a hard time believing it. Anyways, after I told them about the doctors I had seen and the medication I had been taking I think that they started to believe me.

After they realized that this was for real, my friends did something unexpected; they acted as if I had never told them anything. They treated me no differently than they had the entire time I have known them. I believe that may have been key in my recovery. It was my one link to my past self. It helped me to find the person that I was.

Another person who greatly helped my recovery is my friend Britt. I met Britt after I fell into my depression. She was in several of my classes and she would always talk to me. Our relationship grew through the fall semester at school. Britt saw something in me that I did not see in myself, something that I did not understand. No matter how many times we had plans and I broke them because I was not feeling good she was always there. It was not until recently that I told Britt that I was suffering from depression. She was very supportive of me; and would just listen to me talk about how I was feeling. Britt was one of the first people who I told about this book. She was encouraging and helped me through the process. She would read the chapters as I wrote them and provide me with feedback.

In addition to being a friend, Britt helped give me the confidence that I needed to know that I would be okay reentering the social scene. Before I met Britt I did not think that I was worth anyone's time. I could not understand why a person would want to become friends with someone like me. Britt helped me learn to love myself again as well as allowing myself to love others again.

PART III
My Advice

Ways to Deal

After reading my story of denial, diagnosis, treatment, second opinions and recovery; I hope that if you or someone you know is suffering from depression you have learned at least one thing, that you are not alone. Depression is a very common disorder among all ages. There are many causes of depression and there are equally as many ways to deal with it.

One really effective way that I have found in dealing with depression is writing through it. When you are able to write down your feelings, you not only are able to express what you are feeling but you are also able to track your progress. I wrote periodically during my battle with depression, simply to express my feelings. However, throughout my treatment I kept a journal much more regularly; this really helped me to understand how I was progressing. Included below are several entries from my treatment journal:

Journal #1

It is now 5:30 am and I am still unable to fall asleep. I got up and decided to read a book. I read the entire book, 203 pages, in three hours. I am still not tired. I can't believe that I am really unable to sleep. How long is this going to go on? How many more sleepless nights am I going to have to face? I don't know how much more of this I can take

Journal #2

Today I went to talk to Dr. Torello about how I have been feeling. And how I was feeling better and now I feel worse. I'm able to focus in school and get work done, however I'm tired and yawing all day long. Yesterday I was in a very bad mood, I was able to function but I was really irritable. I'm thinking about seeing a psychiatrist. Dr. Torello thinks that I should go and get a full analysis. Then if I am still diagnosed with depression we will perhaps find a more suitable medication for me. Dr. Moore has been recommended to me. I called the insurance company and I'm allowed 20 visits in a calendar year. The doctor I am seeing now is Prozac happy. My mom went to him a few weeks after he diagnosed me and he put her on Prozac because she cleans too much. That is when I decided to go and seek a second opinion.

Journal #3

I know that I'll get better. I just don't want to ruin any relationships or waste my college years being depressed and untreated. I know that everything will be okay it's just a matter of time; and I know I'm in good hands.

Journal #4

Today I turned 21! I went out to dinner with my friends and I got to have a margarita; it was pretty good. Tomorrow night I am going to the bar. I love my friends so much; they're so good to me.

Journal #5

Today I went to lunch with my Aunt Edie. We reminisced about the past, it was a good time. Then I went tanning and to the pharmacy. I got a call from Dr. Moore's office today and I was able to get in early. I found out that I am depressed, and that the dose I was taking was overdosing me. Dr. Moore lowered my dosage and he said that I should start feeling better within about a week. After all this I went out with my friends to the bars. It was fun to see everyone, and to have that experience.

Journal #6

I'm really starting to feel better. I'm a lot more awake during the day. Today I actually felt hungry. I went out to dinner with my sister Kaylee and I had French onion soup, chicken and cheese quesadillas, and a margarita. I have not felt like eating for about two months, the food tasted so good. Also, the muscles spasms that I have been having are almost gone. So physically I'm feeling much better. Psychologically am feeling a little better. I want to be around other people but only for a short amount of time. I have been feeling extremely uncomfortable being around people because I never know what to say to them. Although lately I've been able to talk about anything and everything. Overall I'm feeling pretty well; much better than I was.

Journal #7

Today I feel really bad. My mood is very negative. I don't understand this, I was feeling so good and now this sudden turnaround. I don't think that I can feel this way very long before I really lose my mind. I actually feel worse now than I have the whole entire time that I have been depressed. I think that I'll wait one more day to see if I start feeling any better, and then I'm going to call Dr. Moore.

Journal #8

Today I feel just as bad as I did yesterday. I called Dr. Moore and he told me that he knew that this might happen. He decided to change my dosage from 10 mg to 15 mg. He said that he believed that 10 mg was not a high enough dose for me. He thought that 15 mg would be my therapeutic dose. I am going to go back and see him on in a few days; so I guess we will discuss my progress then.

Journal #9

Today I went to see Dr. Moore. He asked me some questions and told me that he thought that 15 mg was in fact the therapeutic dosage for me. He said that everything was looking good, and that he wanted to see me back when the season changes so we can reevaluate things.

Journal #10

Today Mike really upset me. I really thought that he understood what I am going through. We were discussing the time we spend with our friends. I told him how sometimes when we are with his friends I feel awkward and I want to leave. He does not understand how I feel lonely and I want to be around people; but that when I am around people I feel anxious. I don't really know if it's a lack of understanding, or that I still hide some things from him. He told me that I never told him how I feel anxious in social situations. Either way I think that he is having a hard time supporting me. I think that he wants to get on with his life as a college student and that my problems are holding him back. This is causing problems in our relationship.

I don't want to hold him back; but I really think that I can get over my anxiety by putting myself in situations that make me anxious. The only problem is that when it becomes too much I want to leave. He thinks that if we leave, he is letting his friends down. I don't know who's right, but I would like his support.

As much as I thought Mike understood me, I am beginning to think that he does not. I believe that he acts like he knows what I am going through, and to some degree he may, but I am starting to believe that even though he has been there through all of this he can never fully understand. Perhaps it is wrong of me to expect him to understand. Maybe I need to let him be a college student and just deal with not being a part of that with him.

Journal #11

Today I went back to the campsite that I worked at last sum-
mer. I walked around a lot of the site, just taking in every-
thing. It was very emotional; I tried my best to not cry. I have
been feeling a lot better now and I am really happy that I went
back to the camp. It was very healing for me. I think that it has
given me the closure that I needed.

In addition to keeping a journal another thing that I found very helpful was to talk with people about what I was going through. I found that I felt a lot better when I told people how I had been feeling. I felt that when people understood what I had been going through I would be able to have a bad day around them and they would understand. I did not have to worry about pretending to be happy around people after they knew that I had been suffering from depression. Also after talking to people about my experience with depression I learned that I was not alone. Many people that I spoke with had also battled depression. Three of the women that I work with had experienced depression. I was very surprised to learn about their experiences, but I was also happy to I find people that I could talk with who truly understood what I was going through. Finding someone who is truly empathetic is unbelievably helpful when you need someone to talk to.

Advice

Through my experience with depression, I would like to offer some advice. I should caution you that I am not a doctor and this should not be taken as medical advice, but take my words as you would from a friend who is concerned for you.

DO NOT WAIT

My number one piece of advice is *Do Not Wait.* If you or a loved one feels depressed don't wait to seek medical attention. When I look back at my experience I realize that I waited five months before seeking any type of medical attention. One of the first things that my doctor asked me was, "Why did you wait so long?" When I tried to answer this question I had no good answer. I really don't know why I waited so long. I could have started feeling better so much sooner.

DO NOT FEEL ASHAMED OR ALONE

This was probably my second mistake; I did not tell anyone how I was feeling on the inside because I felt ashamed and alone. I did not think that depression was as common as it is and I really felt ashamed. I was a person who always had control of my own life. When I fell into depression I lost that sense of control, and I did not know what to do. I felt very alone and I also felt ashamed that I had lost control of my own life. I did not understand how this could happen. Just know that if you or a loved one falls into depression, you are not alone and there is nothing to be ashamed of.

IT IS OKAY TO SEEK A SECOND OPINION

I think that this is very important. Yes, doctors have gone through an overwhelming amount of education to become doctors. However they are not all equally trained in every field. Dr. Torello said something to me made a lot of sense so I am going to pass it on, "You would not go to your general practitioner to have a major surgery would you?" The only reasonable response to that question is "NO!" So then you are to think to yourself, "Maybe I should see a doctor that specializes in depression or mood disorders, if I am suffering from depression." It is okay to go see a general practitioner for a first diagnosis or just to talk about your feelings, but if he or she thinks that there is a problem, they should refer you to a specialist; unless they have special training in treating depression. If your doctor does not send you to a specialist and wants to treat you themselves, know that there is nothing wrong with finding a specialist on your own. If I had not sought a second opinion, it is quite likely that I would still be overdosed on Prozac now.

Prozac has helped me immensely; however, Prozac and I suspect other SSRI's are tricky medications for doctors to prescribe effectively. Finding the therapeutic dosage for each patient can be a daunting task. In addition to prescribing the medications, finding the right time to take a patient off of Prozac can be equally daunting. Although I did not write about this anywhere else, I would like to note that when I went off of Prozac, I experienced withdrawal. I became extremely dizzy and as a result nauseated. I was never told that I may experience withdrawal, as I later found out that it is very rare, but after some of my own research and conversations with professionals in the field everyone agreed that I was in fact going through withdrawal. For these reasons I believe that it is very important to find a doctor who listens to you and helps you deal with all of the side effects of any medication that they prescribe; if this means finding another doctor so-be-it.

KNOW HOW YOU FEEL

It is very important to pay attention to how you are feeling. That is one of the reasons that I suggest keeping a journal. Even when you are being treated successfully things can change. I have already changed my dosage four times before we got it right; and I suspect that it will change again. Sometimes a dosage can work for a while and then something happens, maybe in your environment, and your dosage needs changed. The amount of sunlight in a day was adding to the effects of my medication and because of this interaction, I needed to lower my dosage. Just know that if you were being treated successfully and then, all of the sudden or even over some time, you start to feel worse, chances are you're not crazy, you just need your dosage changed. If you start feeling worse don't wait to see if you start feeling better, call your doctor, sometimes they can even change your prescription over the phone. The sooner you call your doctor, the sooner you will feel better.

SURROUND YOURSELF WITH A GOOD SUPPORT GROUP

When I say surround yourself with a good support group; I don't mean that you need to go and find a support group. I should not however, discount support groups, some people may find them very helpful. You can surround yourself with family and friends who are supportive of you. In talking to the people who are close to you; you can work through your feelings. In addition to helping you work through you feelings, they can help you find the medical attention that you may need. I have found that the key to recovery is having good friends, family, and doctors combine together to build a strong support system for you.

TALK WITH PEOPLE YOU TRUST ABOUT YOUR FEELINGS

In addition to surrounding yourself with people that care about you and support you, talk with them about what you are going through. You may be surprised to learn about how many people have either experienced depression, or have helped a loved one cope with depression. I have found it very helpful to talk with others who truly understand what I am going through.

APPENDIX A

Depression

According to Donald F. Klein, M.D, and Paul H. Wender, M.D., authors of *Understanding Depression 2nd ed.*(2005), one in five women and one in ten men will experience depression sometime throughout his or her life. Depression can affect anyone, of any age, of any social class, of any race or ethnic group. Many people will either be faced with depression themselves or have to support a loved one who becomes depressed. Knowing that depression affects so many people, it is very important that people understand what depression is and how it can be treated.

According to Keith Kramlinger, M.D., editor and chief of *Mayo Clinic on Depression* (2002), depression has many causes. Depression can be caused by genetics, stress, chemical dependency, prescription medications, medical conditions, psychological issues and mental illness. Depending on the cause of the onset of depression, treatment may differ. For example, if the cause of depression is biological, the treatment may likely be medications. There are several different classes of antidepressants: selective serotonin reuptake inhibitors also known as SSRI's, mixed reuptake inhibitors, receptor blockers, reuptake inhibitors and receptor blockers, and enzyme inhibitors also known as MAOI's. All of these medications alter the way the brain processes different neurotransmitters.

Psychotherapy may be used as a means to treat depression that was onset due to psychological issues. Psychotherapy comes in many different forms, where the doctor talks with the patient about his or her feelings, and may attempt to alter the way that the patient thinks about things. Also family members may be included in these therapy sessions.

Another type of treatment that has been deemed highly effective in cases of severe depression is electroconvulsive therapy, or ECT. Here the patient is subjected to induced seizures, under anesthetic, that are carefully monitored by a team of trained specialist. The patient must have treatment sessions about three times a week, for two to four weeks. It is not known for sure why ECT works; but it has been shown to be highly effective.

For seasonal affective disorder (SAD), a seasonal depression, light therapy may be used as a means of treatment. Again it is not fully understood how light therapy works but it is thought that light can alter levels of the neurotransmitter serotonin in the brain.

Some other treatments are still somewhat experimental in nature. These include transcranial magnetic stimulation or TMS. TMS is used as a way to stimulate the brain without inducing a seizure. Another experimental treatment is vagal nerve stimulation or VNS. Through a surgical procedure the vagal nerve is stimulated via electrical impulses. This procedure was originally used in patients with epilepsy to help control seizures. Doctors noticed an improvement in mood of the patients who underwent VNS.

In addition to the causes of depression there are many different types and degrees of depression. One type of depression is major depressive disorder, also known as MDD. MDD is what is commonly thought of as depression. A low mood, thoughts of suicide…ect. Another type of mood disorder is manic depression, which is where the patient experiences times of extreme lows and extreme highs. Another type of depression is dysthmia. Dysthmia is very similar to MDD; the symptoms are similar but with dysthmia the symptoms are not as severe. Even though the symptoms are not as strong they last longer than in MDD. In dysthmia symptoms may last for at least two years.

Depression is a very complex disorder; with many causes, levels of severity, and treatments. It is very important to seek proper medical attention.

APPENDIX B

Resources

I wanted to provide some information about depression from the psychiatric and psychological aspect. The provided information comes directly from the National Institute of Mental Health also known as NIMH. And can be found at http://www.nimh.nih.gov/publicat/index.cfm. *Journey Through Darkness* is in no way associated with or endorsed by the NIMH.

How common is depression?

In any given 1-year period, 9.5 percent of the population, or about 18.8 million American adults, suffer from a depressive illness.

What is a depressive disorder?

A depressive disorder is an illness that involves the body, mood, and thoughts. It affects the way a person eats and sleeps, the way one feels about oneself, and the way one thinks about things. A depressive disorder is not the same as a passing blue mood. It is not a sign of personal weakness or a condition that can be willed or wished away. People with a depressive illness cannot merely "pull themselves together" and get better. Without treatment, symptoms can last for weeks, months, or years. Appropriate treatment, however, can help most people who suffer from depression.

How does depression differ in individual experiences?

Not everyone who is depressed experiences every symptom. Some people experience few symptoms, some many. Severity of symptoms varies with individuals and varies over time.

Symptoms of Depression

- *Persistent sad, anxious, or "empty" mood*
- *Feelings of hopelessness, pessimism*
- *Feelings of guilt, worthlessness, helplessness*
- *Loss of interest or pleasure in hobbies and activities that were once enjoyed, including sex*
- *Decreased energy, fatigue, being "slowed down"*
- *Difficulty concentrating, remembering, making decisions*
- *Insomnia, early-morning awakening, or oversleeping*
- *Appetite and/or weight loss or over eating and weight gain*
- *Thoughts of death or suicide; suicide attempts*
- *Restlessness, irritability*
- *Persistent physical symptoms that do not respond to treatment, such as headaches, digestive disorders, and chronic pain*

How is depression diagnosed and treated?

The first step to getting appropriate treatment for depression is a physical examination by a physician. Certain medications as well as some medical conditions such as a viral infection can cause the same symptoms as depression, and the physician should rule out these possibilities through examination, interview, and lab tests. If a physical cause for the depression is ruled out, a psychological evaluation should be done, by the physician or by referral to a psychiatrist or psychologist.

A good diagnostic evaluation will include a complete history of symptoms, i.e., when they started, how long they have lasted, how severe they are, whether the patient had them before and if so, whether the symptoms were treated and what treatment was given. The doctor should ask about alcohol and drug use, and if the patient has thoughts of death or suicide. Further, a history should include questions about whether other family members have had a depressive illness and, if treated, what treatments they may have received and which were effective.

Last, a diagnostic evaluation should include a mental status examination to determine if speech or thought patterns or memory have been affected, as sometimes happens in the case of depressive illness.

Treatment choice will depend on the outcome of the evaluation. There are a variety of antidepressant medications and psychotherapies that can be used to treat depressive disorders. Some people with milder forms may do well with psychotherapy alone. People with moderate to severe depression most often benefit from antidepressants. Most do best with combined treatment: medication to gain relatively quick symptom relief and psychotherapy to learn more effective ways to deal with life's problems, including depression. Depending on the patient's diagnosis and severity of symptoms, the therapist may prescribe medication and/or one of the several forms of psychotherapy that have been proven effective for depression.

Medications

Patients often are tempted to stop medication too soon. They may feel better and think they no longer need the medication. Or they may think that the medication isn't helping at all. It is important to keep taking medication until it has had a chance to work, though the side effects may appear before antidepressant activity does. Once the individual is feeling better, it is important to continue the medication for at least 4 to 9 months to prevent a recurrence of the depression.
** The NIMH notes that some medications must be stopped gradually to give the body time to adjust. **Never** stop taking an antidepressant without*

consulting the doctor for instructions on how to safely discontinue the medication.

What side effects are associated with tricyclic antidepressants and what can be done to deal with them?

- **Dry Mouth** *it is helpful to drink sips of water; chew sugarless gum; clean teeth daily.*

- **Constipation** *bran cereals, prunes, fruit, and vegetables should be in the diet.*

- **Bladder problems** *emptying the bladder may be troublesome, and the urine stream may not be as strong as usual; the doctor should be notified if there is marked difficulty or pain.*

- **Sexual problems** *sexual functioning may change; if worrisome, it should be discussed with the doctor.*

- **Blurred vision** *this will pass soon and will not usually necessitate new glasses.*

- **Dizziness** *rising from the bed or chair slowly is helpful.*

- **Drowsiness as a daytime problem** *this usually passes soon. A person feeling drowsy or sedated should not drive or operate heavy equipment. The more sedating antidepressants are generally taken at bedtime to help sleep and minimize daytime drowsiness.*

The newer antidepressants have different types of side effects:

- **Headache** *this will usually go away*

- **Nausea** *this is also temporary, but even when it occurs, it is transient after each dose.*

- **Nervousness and insomnia (trouble falling asleep or waking often during the night)** *these may occur during the first few weeks; dosage reductions or time will usually resolve them.*

- ***Agitation (feeling jittery)*** *if this happens for the first time after the drug is taken and is more than transient, the doctor should be notified.*

- ***Sexual problems*** *the doctor should be consulted if the problem is persistent or worrisome.*

How to help yourself if you are depressed?

Depressive disorders make one feel exhausted, worthless, helpless, and hopeless. Such negative thoughts and feelings make some people feel like giving up. It is important to realize that these negative views are part of the depression and typically do not accurately reflect the actual circumstances. Negative thinking fades as treatment begins to take effect. In the meantime:

- *Set realistic goals in light of the depression and assume a reasonable amount of responsibility.*

- *Break large tasks into small ones, set some priorities, and do what you can as you can.*

- *Try to be with other people and to confide in someone; it is usually better than being alone and secretive.*

- *Participate in activities that may make you feel better.*

- *Mild exercise, going to a movie, a ballgame, or participating in religious, social, or other activities may help.*

- *Expect your mood to improve gradually, not immediately. Feeling better takes time.*

- *It is advisable to postpone important decisions until the depression has lifted. Before deciding to make a significant transition—change jobs, get married or divorced—discuss it with others who know you well and have a more objective view of your situation.*

- *People rarely "snap out of" a depression. But they can feel a little better day-by-day.*

- *Remember, positive thinking will replace the negative thinking that is part of the depression and will disappear as your depression responds to treatment.*

- *Let your family and friends help you.*

How family and friends can help the depressed person

The most important thing anyone can do for the depressed person is to help him or her get an appropriate diagnosis and treatment. This may involve encouraging the individual to stay with treatment until symptoms begin to abate (several weeks), or to seek different treatment if no improvement occurs. On occasion, it may require making an appointment and accompanying the depressed person to the doctor. It may also mean monitoring whether the depressed person is taking medication. The depressed person should be encouraged to obey the doctor's orders about the use of alcoholic products while on medication. The second most important thing is to offer emotional support. This involves understanding, patience, affection, and encouragement. Engage the depressed person in conversation and listen carefully. Do not disparage feelings expressed, but point out realities and offer hope. Do not ignore remarks about suicide. Report them to the depressed person's therapist. Invite the depressed person for walks, outings, to the movies, and other activities. Be gently insistent if your invitation is refused. Encourage participation in some activities that once gave pleasure, such as hobbies, sports, religious or cultural activities, but do not push the depressed person to undertake too much too soon. The depressed person needs diversion and company, but too many demands can increase feelings of failure.

Do not accuse the depressed person of faking illness or of laziness, or expect him or her "to snap out of it." Eventually, with treatment, most people do get better. Keep that in mind, and keep reassuring the depressed person that, with time and help, he or she will feel better.

Where can I get help?

If unsure where to go for help, check the Yellow Pages under "mental health," "health," "social services," "suicide prevention," "crisis interven-

tion services," "hotlines," "hospitals," or "physicians" for phone numbers and addresses. In times of crisis, the emergency room doctor at a hospital may be able to provide temporary help for an emotional problem, and will be able to tell you where and how to get further help.

- *Family doctors*
- *Mental health specialists, such as psychiatrists, psychologists, social workers, or mental health counselors*
- *Health maintenance organizations*
- *Community mental health centers*
- *Hospital psychiatry departments and outpatient clinics*
- *University- or medical school-affiliated programs*
- *State hospital outpatient clinics*
- *Family service, social agencies, or clergy*
- *Private clinics and facilities*
- *Employee assistance programs*
- *Local medical and/or psychiatric societies*

Appendix C

Other Helpful Resources

These resources are provided as a convenience to the reader and do not imply endorsement of *Journey Through Darkness*, therefore I am assume no responsibility for the content or accuracy of the information that these organizations provide.

National Institute of Mental Health

Information Resources and Inquiries Branch
6001 Executive Boulevard
Room 8184, MSC 9663
Ethesda, MD 20892-9663
1-301-443-4513
Website: http://www.nimh.nih.gov
E-mail: nimhinfo@nih.gov

National Alliance for the Mentally Ill

Colonial Place Three
2107 Wilson Blvd, Suite 300
Arlington, VA 22201
1-703-524-7600; 1-800-950-NAMI
Website: http://www.nami.org

Depression and Bipolar Support Alliance

730 N. Franklin, Suite 501
Chicago, IL 60610-7204
1-312-642-0049; 1-800-826-3632
Website: http://www.DBSAlliance.org

National Mental Health Association

2001 N. Beauregard St., 12th floor
Alexandria, VA 22311
1-703-684-7722; 1-800-969-6642
Website: http://www.nmha.org

Suicide and Mental Health Association International

SMHAI
PO Box 702
Sioux Falls, SD 57101-0702
Website: http://suicideandmentalhealthassociationinternational.org

American Psychological Association

750 1st Street, NE
Washington, DC 20002-4242
1-202-336-5510
TollFree: 1-800-374-2721
Website: http://www.apa.org

Depression After Delivery, Inc. (DAD)

91 East Somerset Street
Raritan, NJ 08869
TollFree: (800) 944-4773
Website: http://www.depressionafterdelivery.com

Depression and Related Affective Disorders Association (DRADA)

2330 West Joppa Road, Suite 100
Lutherville, MD 21093
1-410-583-2919
Email: drada@jhmi.edu
Website: http://www.drada.org/

Bibliography

DiGiando, Theresa. Interviewed by author. Gahanna, Ohio, 20 December 2005

Heinmiller, Mike. Interview by author. Gahanna, Ohio, 14 March 2006.

Klein, Donald, M.D., and Paul Wender, M.D. *Understanding Depression 2nd ed.* USA: Oxford University Press, 2005.

Kramlinger, Keith, M.D. Ed. *Mayo Clinic on Depression.* Broomall, 2002.

National Institute of Mental Health. Depression. Bethesda (MD): National Institute of Mental Health, National Institutes of Health, US Department of Health and Human Services; 1994 [2002; cited 2006 June]. (NIH Publication Number: NIH 5124). 23 pages. Available from: http://www.nimh.nih.gov

978-0-595-40537-4
0-595-40537-1